THE
HANUKKAH
STORY

THE HANUKKAH STORY

By Marilyn Hirsh

BONIM BOOKS

New York · London

TO MY PARENTS

Copyright © 1977 by Marilyn Hirsh

Library of Congress Cataloging in Publication Data

Hirsh, Marilyn.
  The Hanukkah story.

  SUMMARY: Relates the struggle of Judah Maccabee and his small army
against the overwhelming might of the Syrians and how this event gave rise to
the celebration of Hanukkah.
  1. Hanukkah (Feast of Lights) — Juvenile literature. 2. Maccabees —
Juvenile literature. [1. Hanukkah (Feast of Lights) 2. Maccabees]
  I. Title.

BM695.H3H57 296.4'35 77-22183

ISBN 0-88482-756-9

BONIM BOOKS

a division of Hebrew Publishing Company
80 Fifth Avenue
New York, N.Y. 10011

Printed in the United States of America

Long ago, the Jews lived in Israel. It was called Judea then. Most of the people were farmers and shepherds. They plowed their fields and took care of their sheep and goats.

Judea had one large and important city called Jerusalem. There, high on a hill, stood the beautiful Holy Temple of the Jewish people.

All Jews came there as often as they could. At harvest time, the farmers came to offer their first fruits to God. Rich people brought gifts of gold and silver.

In those days, the Jews did not rule themselves. Antiochus the Fourth, King of Syria, ruled Judea and some other small countries. But he really wanted to be king of the whole world.

The Jews paid taxes to Antiochus. They didn't bother him and he left them alone—for a while.

But soon, Antiochus decided it was time to conquer more countries.

"I'm going to be Antiochus the Greatest," he bragged. "Everyone I rule must do exactly as I say. I'll conquer more people and make them obey me, too. But I'll need a bigger army and armies cost money."

Then he thought of all the riches in the Temple in Jerusalem. "Aha!" he exclaimed. "I am the King. Jerusalem belongs to me. The Temple is in Jerusalem. The treasure is in the Temple. And so, the treasure is mine!"

The King sent his soldiers to bring him gold and silver from the Temple. But the High Priest, who was in charge of the Temple, would not let them in. So Antiochus sent one of his own friends to be the new High Priest.

"What a lot of gold and silver they have here," said the new High Priest. "I'll send some to the King and I'll keep some for myself. I'm sure no one will miss it."

But, of course, the other priests did miss it and they told everyone. The people were so angry that the High Priest had to surround the Temple with soldiers to protect himself.

Meanwhile, Antiochus was adding more and more soldiers to his army. Soon, he felt ready to conquer more countries.

"I'll start with Egypt," he declared. So, off he went, taking a huge army with him.

Someone in Jerusalem heard that Antiochus had been killed in battle.

"The King is dead," whispered one person to another. Soon everyone knew.

Many Jews rushed to the Temple. "Down with the High Priest!" they shouted.

The High Priest and the soldiers fought the people. While they were fighting, Antiochus surprised everyone by arriving with his army.

He had not been able to conquer Egypt. He was disappointed, but very much alive. When he saw the fighting in Jerusalem, he was also very angry.

"Attack!" he yelled to his soldiers.

The Jews fought back, but they had no leader. They were no match for the Syrian army and many of them were killed.

When Antiochus returned to Syria, he left thousands of his soldiers in Jerusalem. There seemed to be more soldiers than Jews. Unlike the Jews, the Syrians worshipped many gods. The soldiers put statues of their gods in the Holy Temple. The largest statue was of Zeus, king of their gods. His face looked a bit like Antiochus himself.

But this was not enough for Antiochus.

"The trouble all started in the Temple," he thought. "It must be their God. The Jews must stop praying to their God and start praying to my gods."

The King made a Royal Proclamation:

From now on, the Temple will be
called the Temple of Zeus.
All Jews will bow down and offer
sacrifices to Zeus.

Antiochus was ready to put his seal on the proclamation. Then he decided, "The Jews must also stop celebrating their own holidays and studying their own laws."

So he added two more rules:

No Jew may celebrate the Sabbath.
No Jew may study the Torah.

And he signed it,

Antiochus the Fourth

Some Jews ran away from Jerusalem rather than obey the King's rules. Secretly, they continued to study the Torah and pray to God. They wanted to fight back, but they still had no leader.

Syrian soldiers were sent all over Judea. No place was safe.

One day, the soldiers came to the small village of Modi'in, bringing a statue of Zeus. They set it up in the main square with an altar in front of it. They ordered the village elder, Mattathias, to bow down to the statue and sacrifice a pig.

"Never!" cried Mattathias. "I worship the one God—the King of Kings—and I will bow down to no other."

Another man, who was afraid of the soldiers, spoke up. "I will sacrifice to Zeus," he said.

Mattathias was so enraged at this that he killed the man. Then he and his five strong sons attacked the surprised soldiers. All the people of Modi'in joined in the fight. To everyone's amazement, they won.

"We must leave Modi'in," said Mattathias, "but not to hide. The time has come to fight for our land and our Torah. Whoever is for the Lord, follow me!"

"We are with you!" everyone cried.

They took weapons from the fallen soldiers and quickly packed whatever they could carry. By nightfall, the men, women, and children of Modi'in were climbing up to caves in the hills.

All over Judea, people heard of the bravery of Mattathias and his five sons—John, Simon, Judah, Eleazar, and Jonathan.

Many men found their way up into the hills to join them. Gradually, they became an army.

But Mattathias was very old and he was not a soldier. He decided that his son Judah should lead the army.

"You are the strongest of my sons," he told Judah. "You are called the Maccabee, the hammer. Train our people to be hammers, too. Strike the Syrians again and again."

"I will try," Judah promised.

Mattathias died soon after, but the work he started went on.

The men practiced with their swords and shields, bows and arrows. Every day, more men came. Judah decided they must begin to fight.

He called the army together and said, "The Syrians are many and we are few. But, as God helped David win against the giant Goliath, so He will help us.

"When we came here, we were farmers. Now we are the Maccabees.

"We know every hill and rock of our land. We will ambush the enemy soldiers where they least expect us. God will help us and we will win!"

So the surprise attacks began.

The Maccabees won several small battles and captured a lot of Syrian weapons. The Syrians tried to keep Antiochus from finding out. They knew he would be angry. They were right.

When the King learned of Judah's army, he screamed at his officers, "You are idiots! I pay you to win, not to be beaten by farmers. Take whatever you need and don't come back until the Maccabees are defeated!"

The first general sent by the King attacked Judea from the north.
He had a beautiful sword that he always used in battle.

The Maccabees trapped his army in a narrow valley. The Syrians
were crowded so close together and their armor was so heavy that
they could hardly move.

The Maccabees won. Judah captured the beautiful sword. He
used it in battle for the rest of his life.

The next general came along the coast and attacked Judea from the west. He, too, was defeated by the Maccabees.

Antiochus sent more important generals with even larger armies. Two generals went far down the coast to attack from the south. They led an army of thousands of men, with horses, chariots, and even huge elephants with sharp tusks.

This was the biggest battle of all. Judah and his men were greatly outnumbered. The elephants panicked and trampled Jews and Syrians alike. But the Maccabees wouldn't give up. When the fighting was over, they had won.

Antiochus was far away, fighting in another country, when he heard about the Maccabees' victory.

"Why has this flood of trouble come to me?" he moaned.

Not long after, Antiochus fell ill and died. Some say that, before he died, he felt sorry for the way he had treated the Jews.

Now the road to Jerusalem was free. As the Maccabees entered the city, crowds rushed to welcome them. Judah led everyone up the hill and into the Temple courtyard.

The Syrian soldiers had abandoned the Temple. Because they had left the statue of Zeus there, the Jews had not come to the Temple for a long time, either. The gates were broken. The courtyard was filled with weeds and rubbish.

With a great shout, the Maccabees smashed the statue of Zeus.

At once, everyone started cleaning the Temple. They made new ornaments and a gold, seven-branched Menorah. They rebuilt the altar with whole stones, according to the laws of the Torah.

At last, the Temple was ready to be dedicated, to be used again for the worship of God.

The Temple was aglow with light. Gold ornaments sparkled on the gates. Everyone prayed and sang to the music of harps, flutes, and cymbals.

For eight days, more and more Jews came from all over Judea. The courtyard overflowed with happy people.

Judah announced that the dedication of the Temple would be celebrated every year at the same time. The word *Hanukkah* means "dedication." The year was 164 B.C.E., more than 2,100 years ago.

And every year from that time on, Jews all over the world have continued to enjoy the holiday of Hanukkah, lighting a special Menorah for eight days, beginning on the twenty-fifth of the Hebrew month of Kislev.

A story is told about the first Hanukkah. When the Temple was dedicated, no pure oil could be found to light the Menorah. Searching through the Temple, the Maccabees found only one jug of pure oil, untouched by the Syrian soldiers. Even though it was enough oil for just one day, by a miracle, it burned for eight days until new oil could be prepared.

Many people today think that the only miracle of Hanukkah is the miracle of the oil. But, thinking about the story of Judah and the Maccabees, isn't their victory a miracle, too?